I MUST NOT WRITE POEMS ABOUT MY FRIENDS

I MUST NOT WRITE POEMS ABOUT MY FRIENDS

Revised Edition

DEBBY CURREEN

Grumpy Dog Publishing

First published in 2020
@Arkhouse Press, Australia

Copyright © 2024 by Debby Curreen
Grumpy Dog Publishing
Far North, New Zealand

All rights reserved. No part of this book may be reproduced in any manner whatsoever without written permission except in the case of brief quotations embodied in critical articles and reviews.

First Printing, 2024

Contents

	1
INTRODUCTION	2
	4
I must not write poems about my friends	5
	6
Old Friends	7
I will meet you on Quail Ridge	9
I'm so fresh	11
Aunty Slizer from Bach Flower Cottage	13
I love you to the sky, Apple Pie	15
The Pig Farmer's Wife	16
JEWELS	18
The night the tui came for you	20
I'm going to Poetry Jail	22
Family	25

	26
This Is What We Fight For	27
I Wear This Scarf Like Your Love	29
I will write for you, Elaine	31
Heart up a sleeve	33
Tears In Springtime	35
Moments of life	37
	38
Invitation to Marath-On	39
You are the Cure for everything	41
As copacetic as a big Mon on the Bayou	43
Bird, it's a thunder kind of night	45
There are no ghosts here	47
Heroes	49
If Keith Richards died tonight	50
Lord, let me write like Cohen	52
Channelling Virginia Woolf	54
Alice the Villain	56
Angie with the gold heart	58
Soliloquy to Sinead	60
	63

Visit Lyn today (1986)	65
Bon voyage Pikelet (1988)	66
Funny as Pikelets & Donuts (2019)	67
In the stillness I find you God	69
The Light in my Heart	70
ACKNOWLEDGEMENTS	73
About The Author	74

Dedication

For my funny, loyal, colourful, crazy, loving friend –
Linda Armstrong
RIP Pikelet xxx
"For from Allah we come and to Allah we return"

INTRODUCTION

In 2020 I published a collection of poems called, "I must not write poems about my friends". Four years on, I have revised the collection by removing a few (for personal reasons) and adding some new ones (because they are so damn good). I have also changed the cover of this book. So please enjoy this "revised edition".

For almost as long as I can remember, I have written stories and poems about my beloved friends, family, and on occasion, myself.

My first poem about life was at age six and became my first ever, published piece in the school newsletter.

In recent years, when I first started to jot down little ditties poking affectionate fun at my friends, I mostly found nobody was ever offended and often friends seemed to find my little written caricatures to be quite flattering.

Too often though, these days, I write with great love and reminiscence of special times had together or memories of a friend or family member no longer with us.

But mostly a bit of a laugh is had, and all poems have been written with love and mixed intentions.

Sadly, on Friday 15 March 2019, I lost one of my closest friends in the Christchurch Mosque shootings. This collection is dedicated to Linda, one of my longest friendships spanning over 40 years which now stretches into eternity until that blessed day we meet again in Glory.

So, watch yourselves around me, behave or if you can't, don't leave pens and bits of blank paper lying around when I am in the room.

God bless y'all and forgive me if you must.

I must not write poems
about my friends

Old Friends

Old friends is a place,
in your heart,
like battered suitcases,
carried from town to town, to home and back.
Full of pictures, laughter, sad times and wine with crackers,
the tears from hard days and nights.
We carry old friends,
never leaving them behind or in a dumpster,
tied up in plastic sacks,
driven away from and never looking back.
We save that for enemies.
Old friends come with us,
wrapped carefully like precious bone china,
stored in the cupboards of our heart and clearly labelled,
Fragile.
One day we find them again,
and we bring them out to wine and dine with again.
We remember, oh we remember and it's still too funny
but not sad, well a bit.
We are grateful that we lived,

to watch another sun set,
over another meal together.
Sitting on the suitcases of our lives,
unwrapping the precious and the fragile,
comforted by the familiar,
sharing the dust of lives thoroughly lived.

I will meet you on Quail Ridge

Whenever I think of you, my friend,
the memories
flood from a heart
of love and times too big
for a special lake to contain.
I remember all the tea and coffee,
the cakes, the muffins and prayers,
the talks and the times of tears.
The days of joyous victories,
Hallelujahs
and dreams that had at last come true.
That's when I think of you.
All those years,
children, marriages,
births and deaths and big, lonely islands
in between.
Then I remember your smile and your voice,
and I miss you.

So that's when I call and I hope,
for just a few hours,
spent in the past,
dreaming of a gentle future,
while we sip our tea and eat our cake,
in a house,
at the top of the magical Quail Ridge xx

I'm so fresh

    I'm so fresh,
with my big fish,
wide grin, loud excuse,
twinkle in my eye,
oh is that the time,
oh my!
    Where did the day
and the night,
the moon and sun,
go with the time.
I could have been there,
with my love on her pillows,
in a bed now cold.

But I'm so fresh,
when I cook your fish,
as you sleep off the anxiety that I sent,
all night long and after the sunset,
as you tossed,
you churned,

AND locked the door, whilst your heart burned.

But my fish is fresh,
my smile stinks,
good intentions down the sink,
cold pillows,
and several hits about the head.
Lucky fish,
    already dead.

And like my love on her pillows,
the moon has sunk,
with my bad excuses;
fried in the setting sun,
burning fillets,
sour chowder.
I'm too late for love on her warm pillows tonight.

Aunty Slizer from Bach Flower Cottage

    Aunty Slizer's cottage,
is a home without a chimney,
and crazy paving lined with herbs,
hidden behind black trees and wild brambles;
as to her door we skip,
anxious to be with Aunty Slizer, the picture painter,
    from Bach Flower Cottage,
    where we eat good things from her pearly shell plates.

She wears a super hero cape;
she made it herself with "SS" for SUPER Slizer on the front,
(not secret service or super-size)
and Aunty Slizer says she has powers,
that she can fly and drive big cars backwards really fast,
and she once wrestled an Orca,
but that's not true, the Orca thing.

She drinks beer made from bark,

that she picks from the trees in the secret forest behind her
water tank,
where white horses run with the rabbits,
beside a stream full of blue frogs,
and multi coloured totara trees sing at night with the birds.
    I love Aunty Slizer from Bach Flower Cottage,
in her super cape of many colours.
She said she is never going to grow up and
we make up songs and sing them out loud in the bath.
Weeks are too short and the nights a bit long,
before each sunny day that I spend with her.
And as I leave her arms, I whisper into her ear,
"I'll be back and one day, I will never leave you and
we will sing songs forever on the back of an orca,
and I will wear my cape and have a big E on my heart that's
stands for - Ever."

I love you to the sky, Apple Pie

If someone asks, how much I love you,
this is what I say without hesitation,
with all my heart,
while I give a big loud shout,
using my biggie-est, homiest voice-
"I love you to the sky, Apple Pie."
Not up by the moon,
drifting round anonymous stars,
ending up in space cars,
losing it on the Milky Way in a dark and foreign sky.
It's down here on Earth,
my gym shoes on the ground,
raising barbells in the air,
like the beat of my heart in my chest,
and I cry...
"I love you to the sky, Apple Pie,
you really are the best."

The Pig Farmer's Wife

"Oink, oink, oink," the silly girl laughs,
running up the path,
banging on the door of her lover's grubby house,
set amongst pens of pigs,
with puddles of stinky mud.
"Oink, oink. I'm home,"
she calls,
to her smelly, pig farmer beau.
Behind her,
a home of comfort and her mother's tears,
fall down faster than a hurricane's rain in winter.
You can laugh now,
grown up lady,
at your story,
the close call you had,
at being a Pig Farmer's wife,
who squealed from all the roly-poly love at night,
to then sleep all day like a pig in mud.
Until you awoke one morning
to hear consequences beating at your door, and

there stood parents, education, real job and more.
So much more,
on that reckoning day,
when they lead you back to reality,
and away from the path where you had strayed,
albeit with glee,
the odours of fun
clinging to your clothes,
as up a perfect garden path
cuffed to the hands of love and family,
who, dragging your rebellious body,
led you back to perfumed reality.
Your dreams of love,
hopes of matrimony
and becoming the Missus of a pig farmer,
were hosed away like the stench of a pig pen,
closed up and as abandoned as a butchery on World Vegetarian Day...whew!
You almost had it made.

JEWELS

In a high school,
far, far away from comfort and class
we met in a secret location
hidden from teacher's prying eyes,
and detention pads...
sharing cigarettes and swearing about our next interminable class.
Teetering like a mudslide,
inside that dreary mausoleum of fractured learning,
where pupils eschewing social graces
in favour of short skirts and heavy eye make-up,
forbidden earrings and the wrong-coloured socks.
We hid from "the Duck",
running from "Ol' Ma Miller,"
where days ended as we piled into rattling old buses for escape.
We were funny friends,
you and me.
Not serious about school but definite about life.
Leaving the former

diving into the latter.
City jobs and heels,
better buses,
nicer lunches and a loyal friendship forged over weekends.
I plucked you from the Internet years later,
throwing you into my first novel,
as Drag King Elton,
gifted, successful and scary.
A fitting re-entry for a decade's old friendship,
forged on a hill, coated in rebellion,
layered with memories and amusement well forged with love.

The night the tui came for you

The sun is bright and a soft wind blows calmly through your window,
I say, "Listen to that singing outside, what can it be?"
"It's the tuis,' you say,
"they're waiting for me."
"But not today," I said, and you laughed with me,
"not today, I'm not ready, they will have to wait."
I agreed, no one was ready yet, and you stayed for a while longer.
They returned the next day, and the next,
those tuis sang together,
and we came to enjoy their boisterous chorus.
"They're still here," I told you.
"Yes," you said, "but it's sunny, so they can just stay in the trees and cry,"
We laughed together, as we watched the tuis in the kowhai,
harmonising together,
in the branches that touched the sky.

I MUST NOT WRITE POEMS ABOUT MY FRIENDS

I stand over you, some days later,
the sky was grey and the clouds hung lower than broken hearts,
you were gone,
leaving us quietly, in the early morn.
I looked in the kowhai but the tuis were also gone.
You had beaten them at their own waiting game-
you dodged their songs,
for in the light before dawn you had gone.
I had to have a little laugh,
and I sang a quiet song.
You have gone but you'll never be forgotten,
you have left memories, colourful and strong.
And together we outwitted the tuis,
they were too late, the night they came for you,
angels bet them too it,
while I slept deeply next to you.
Now you'll listen to the birdsong in heaven,
yes you will.
But I am going to miss you,
while that kowhai tree stands still;
and at night when I am all alone,
I cry softly and sing adieu,
then chuckle to myself about how you fled,
the night the tui's came for you.

I'm going to Poetry Jail

I'm off to join the convicts,
because I know I'm going to jail.
I know I promised myself and the world,
I wouldn't write poems about any friend,
but I have,
I just can't help myself,
so poetry jail will be my end.
I hope to make new friends in there,
someone new to write about.
I hope my words will make them sing and laugh,
and dance and jump about.
I hope I don't upset anyone,
I don't want to get thrown out.
Because where do you go after jail,
when you can no longer stay,
where do the fallen poets go,
when their words cause outrage and dismay.
Is there a dark and dreary dungeon,
where ostracised wordsmiths dwell?
A place to sit and mutter,

a room that smells like hell.
Even though my subjects were anonymous,
you could still guess their names,
I always new my verses were dicey,
but I still played that tricky, slippery game.
My editor tried to warn me,
but her words sailed straight past my ear,
"people can get upset,
so stop making fun of them with your words,
I'm warning you for the final time,
to please, please do beware."
Of course, I bloody ignored her words,
I paid her warning little heed,
casting silly words around,
until they all caught up with me,
so now I'm going to bleed.
For finally I've written something,
and the person did not find it funny,
that I'd dramatized their misfortune
And even made some money.
"Well, that's what paparazzi do,"
I said in my defence,
"You hypocrites who laugh at other people,
from the safe side of your fence."
I'm being charged with sarcasm,
and also, mirth and slander.
As well as trying to bribe the judge,
Who refused my generous backhander.
So off I go to Poetry Prison.

I'm being locked up for a year,
they're denying me internet, pens and paper,
for my entire time in there.
They're going to be bloody sorry,
when I finally get out,
because I'll hide behind a non-de plume
and use the internet to troll, and curse and laugh at,
all those stuffy fudgers that I missed out.

Family

This Is What We Fight For

I wake in a morning of wind and grey,
I hope, and this is what I pray,
Lord, roll the darkness back today.
Make all turmoil sink deep,
in the water of your love,
the sea of forgetfulness,
as falling into Baptism,
the souls of my sons,
I commit to you to keep.
For this is what I fought for, to see,
you call me out upon the deep water, Lord;
and I would come.
Please take my hand, God, as I tumble from a rocking boat,
into large and foaming waves,
defying a life that growls
and taunts me, beckoning me and laughing,
"Come, my quiet one," I hear your call.
"Help me stand up, Lord," I answer.
"to walk alone across the sea,
to just be with you."

Call me out of the boat, Lord,
make me leave the dead behind.
All that is safe and warm,
I will cast aside,
just to glimpse your face,
through churning, frothy white horses of salty brine.
As every darkness splashes at our sides,
falling at our feet,
as I step across that ocean,
and behind the waves we will meet.
I would give up tequila for you,
just for a second,
so I could get to see my sons go down in to a lake of shame,
to see them rise again.
Leave me to fight, Lord,
I will do it alone,
and let the sun rise and set forever, but I will wait.
Never forget that I will call God's warriors to pray and hedge over me,
and then when we have stood and all is done,
I will kick that dry earth and stale air,
to see my sons rise up in Your hands,
out of a river of loss,
into a bright Glory day,
with a past buried far behind.
I will fight for all of this,
and give up everything just to see
my sons shine on a dull November day.

I Wear This Scarf Like Your Love

I wear this scarf,
every day around my neck,
like your love, it drapes around me and keeps me warm,
on days of little sun.
At night I hang this mantle of your care,
a watchman over my dreams,
the guard upon my life,
silk falling above my head as I softly breathe beneath your love.
Every day, I search out this scrap of you,
twining comfort and memory against my throat,
thinking of you, not so far away,
but not here with me.
Wishing to see your smiling face and
hear you laugh about just how stink a life can turn,
and without you, all seems dark.
Sometimes if not for your phone calls,
constant and hoped for,

my days would go on forever.
Watch me hold this slip of silken love,
that you have delivered to me,
unbidden as it falls against my breast,
I can breathe,
knowing you are with me,
wrapping me in this wispy gift.
(Mothers Day 2017)

I will write for you, Elaine

Come to me,
come to Taipa.
My darling,
I will write for you.
On the beach,
inside the waves of home
and by the love
we grew up with.
Our eyes will water,
at the memories
of everyone,
we have held in our arms,
now heavy
with good-byes.
Come down to the ocean,
the surges of life that rush over sand,
coating hearts with vision,
of tomorrows to share, and
the yesterdays
now locked down with gold.

Wrap me in your arms,
let's share heart breathe,
as I write for you,
beside a foaming sea of joy,
waves rolling on forever.

Mightier than the waves of the sea, is His love for you (and me)

Heart up a sleeve

    He keeps his heart up his sleeve,
that one.
Not much noise,
no drama...
plays a song and sings out loud like,
it was written for him and all about,
his love gone bad,
so sad,
frayed sleeves hiding a heart breaking.

Long gone kindred spirits,
left you nothing but blank walls to bounce,
off your,
words and cries,
life and real stuff from a heart full,
falling silent and shrinking back,
into ...

Sleeves pulled down like shades in the day.
Sitting silent, waiting, looking out into a sky full of blue,

watching for,
and waiting for a love.
A Heart sits on a table beating,
listening,
speaking to an air full of empty,
quiet and slowly fraying.

"I'd rather keep my heart up my sleeve on a warm day, than risk the shadows of loneliness that lurk beneath every pavement," said The Man.

Tears In Springtime

In Spring
I always remember the friends of yesterday
gathered around a coffee table
spiked with jasmine
flush with freesias
in the days when cigarettes didn't kill you.
    We all smoked and drank strong instant coffee
full of harmless sugar
cups and ashtrays brimming over
like the love we held for each other.
    Perfumed, smoky, strong...
that's how I remember us.

Moments of life

Invitation to Marath-On

This is a special invitation
for you my active friend.
I want you to come on a marathon;
it's 26 miles to the end.
You'll need to give up smoking
and increase your caffeine intake.
You'll have to whip up your metabolism
'cause there's fame and fortune at stake.

You'll have to get up every morning,
at least three hours before dawn.
We have to do some intensive training -
more than a run round the lawn.
It's time to start building up muscle and
whittling fat cells away.
It's a diet of lean meat and brown rice
you can throw all your Tim Tams away.
Your running attire is all lycra
with a crop top that's pink and says, "RUN".

When we cool down from rigorous training,
our motto will be, "THIS IS FUN."

    Oh yes my dear friend, Helen,
you'll become a smoke-free zone.
We'll pull the Fletcher Challenge off
and take the trophy home.
I will keep the prize money,
for as your trainer, I am the real star.
So don't think for a moment that I'm running with you,
I'll be following you in your car.

You are the Cure for everything

I see storms and
I throw myself into the arms
of your quiet love
that blocks wind
and rain,
driving away pain.
I seek shelter
from life
and myself,
the long days that make me cry,
into the nights,
but when you are here
I find myself sighing,
as I let go of my frightened breathe.
I don't doubt tomorrow,
when you are in it.
You,
the cure for everything.

The missing music,
flowers in my heart,
the strong arms in the dark nights that I long for...
your kind smile in a fresh morning.
Everything I ever lost,
all the moments,
I wish to forget,
fade into whispery dusks,
when beside me,
you make everything all right,
a heavenly cure that heals my life.

As copacetic as a big Mon on the Bayou

Cracking crawfish,
sinking Johnnie Walker,
bombs away,
till the pinkness of a new dawn creeps over a river of Life.
Banishing ghosts of ancestors,
as a sun rises over willows sweeping the days gone by.
Make me as copacetic as humble pie,
brimming with cream,
spilling the fruits of our labours,
that buried the shame of too much excess,
the nights forgotten,
down by the banks of sunsets lost.
Let copacetic reign on a new day full of mercy.
I am excellent, in order,
seething with life,
screaming a pardon of love over the waves of dread.
Crushing spite,
spitting bullets,

hoping against death that another day will arise,
to sink transgressions beneath barrels of pain,
for I am...copacetic as a big Mon,
noble as an Oak on the Big Bayou.

Bird, it's a thunder kind of night

(*For Taipa*)
Bird, it's a Thunder kind of night.
All red leather on those hot seats,
behind a left-hand drive, with you beside me.
Any old Bat mobile would do
 but this black beast would take us into a night
beside a beach of dreams,
crashing into loud heartbeats,
snug hugs
just you and me.
It's a black Thunder night bird,
and I miss you.
I would ride with you across yellow lines
on red leather,
 while lightning clouds and gale force wind chases us into rich valleys of surprise,
  spitting gravel on roads that drop into river pools,
  that have caught all the times I spent with you.

Buckle me in beside that left hand drive,
alongside the tattoos of your love for me.
Let's steer our souls into the darkness,
one more time,
because it's a thunder kind of night, Bird.

There are no ghosts here

I drift through the winding Jasmine,
like we used to in the "old days",
when I enjoyed having moonlight strolls by a river with you.
Morning brought crepes and lemon sauce,
car rides in a clapped out Austin,
hitchhiking at night in the winter,
living in a funny little bach,
and then a half-finished house...
these fragments in my mind that have now become ghosts to me,
when the days were made of peppermint chip ice cream
and all of it spent with you.
I make my way back to all the "spots",
up roads, down streets, walking narrow lanes and on a people-less seashore.
I asked a woman about you and visited a man who knew you,
then I found the orchard beside the pond where we'd lived
but everything had changed.
The pictures in my mind bubbled to the top of a lake
I once called forgetfulness,

then I swam in the sea of forgiveness for myself.

"There are no ghosts here," I said to a stranger walking by, with a spaniel dog.

" Good day for it," he nodded to me.

"I think I'll go home now," I told the dashing clouds above my head.

I waited for the ghosts to whisper, "Stay."

I watched the sunset at Ruby Bay.

I went back to my rented cabin,

and I sent my love a text..."There are no ghosts here...they're all gone."

He sent this message back to me...

"I miss you."

I waited for the sun to rise over Ruby Bay,

I missed him too, and then I said good-bye to the ghosts,

and getting on a place,

I whispered, "I'm coming back" to everything and, of course, to you.

Heroes

If Keith Richards died tonight

If Keith Richards died tonight...
I would hang upside down from a tree,
over a smouldering pile of Marlboro ciggies and scream,
out loud for everyone to hear,
"Start me up."
It's a new year,
14 days in, two weeks and not many rock star deaths,
not big stars,
not immortal shooting babes,
like an old fart called Keith.
The news of the world is quiet,
and maybe death has taken a holiday,
summer, winter and all days,
and nights with a full moon or less.
I just hope Keith Richards doesn't die,
not just yet,
because he's just so clever,
as he plays that guitar like handsome dogs at midnight,

howling among shadows,
crying out from hearts gone lonely,
calling for some sunlight and fresh flowers,
to mix with steaming coffee.
Keith, don't die tonight,
there's still a lot of day,
a lot of light and I can hear a Rolling Stones song playing,
loud and pure, and something else...
honky, tonkity wisps,
from a smoky, juke joint bar,
because anywhere in the world right now, Keith,
it's whiskey o'clock.
Cheers!!!
I hope you live forever, man xxx

Lord, let me write like Cohen

I don't want to move like Jagger,
paint like Picasso,
sing like Elvis or...
act like Pacino.
I want to write like Cohen!
I don't want to ride like a Crusty Demon,
dance like Ginger,
act like Marilyn,
croon like Sinatra and drink like Dean.
Just give me a pen so I can write like Cohen.
Let me make you cry,
make you swoon and sigh,
sing to sad songs,
remembering every lost love at sunrise.
As you wipe your eyes,
while my words punch your heart,
writing like Cohen,
tearing you apart.

I MUST NOT WRITE POEMS ABOUT MY FRIENDS - 53

His searing, searing words,
sung by famous, famous people,
in block- busting, busting, show stopping movies.
Singing and strumming and crooning,
making y'all a swooning.
Bending the breeze,
sipping whisky,
shooting stars.
God love 'im.
I want to be just like him,
the Gangster of Prose.
Please God,
let me write just one poem,
or a single song just as good as Cohen.

Channelling Virginia Woolf

I have been channelling Virginia Woolf,
the words,
not the spirit
because I live far too close
to a river,
to let that dumb shit guide me,
past pocket-sized rocks,
down well-worn paths,
beside the sucking tide.
No, not the spirit of Virginia
the writing.
I channel Virginia Woolf, stanzas,
picky sonnets of tepid days,
and darkened rooms by night,
starless, hopeless,
sunny respite,
amidst the settling ash of winter fires,
my words are lively,

in small part, and thanks I think,
Virginia.

Alice the Villain

(from the tv series "Luther")
Send me a text
then don't call back.
Leave me hanging like,
thorny berries on some wild vine,
untended,
overripe and waiting for a hot sun,
that burns my quivering lips.
Call me and say,
"I'm missing you.
Where are you?"
Let me say back to you,
"Here. Alone.
Cold and shaking,
where you left me."
I want you back
to top up my repertoire of pain,
with your long charms,
and wrap me up in your smile,
whisper warm promises into my doubting ears,

stroke my twitching skin.
But oh, those warm words!
They all go cold,
in the dust of your foot steps,
as they fall to the ground in
front of me,
whilst I wait for your non-return.
There we have it, again,
my topped-up repertoire of pain,
stinging like the salty tears
dropping on my bed coverlet
as my heart
breaks into my shaking hands,
drowning out your non-goodbye.

Angie with the gold heart

There are some friends,
from many years gone back,
40 to be exact.
They stay, and forgive,
they never forget,
you ring them up after months for a chat...well,
Angie's like that.
You talk fun on the phone,
hours and hours at a time,
the minutes fly
while words shoot forth
like sparks in the dark from a furnace,
where diamonds are forged,
as every day we carry with us,
those pearls we paid for with the highest price.
Yes, we sweated our hearts out for that, and
time after time,
Angie's always like that.
Like summer's song,
Angie's kitchen calls to me at dawn,

delicious coffee, leads to scones,
the latest fruit jam of the season,
often straight for the pot join
salad, meats and whacky, cracky wholemeal bread.
Then we're moving into winter,
soups and teas of herbs,
grown at her back door,
so much more,
all mixed up with love besides purring fires,
sleeping cats.
Angie's home is full of that.
We all sleep beside a river,
lulled by it's night-time burble.
I hear Angie's prayers,
drift glowing and purple,
across the night and into our hearts,
weaving, mending,
cementing, protecting,
all our lives,
she holds us tight,
she never gives up.
Angie's always like that.

Soliloquy to Sinead

I will go down to the beach today,
down to the sea on those craggy rocks
to stare the waves down,
dip my toes in ice cold pacific blue water,
to dream for a while and remember you.
I will walk alone across the chilly rocks,
and stare at a silent ocean that shivers and roils,
at the time and tide that is waiting for me.
I will find the darkest rock to perch on and hold your life in my arms,
as memories of you gather around me,
singing to me in time with the gentle waves lapping at my feet,
while the pining seagulls drift on the arctic winds of winter overhead,
I imagine the winds blowing down from Ireland today,
I don't know if that's even true.
But this is an ode, and we're Irish,
so we can say whatever we want to.
I will stand by the sea today and watch...

the melding colours of aqua depths, swirl,
unfettered and free, as I write something new in my head,
to take home to the table where I will sit,
and think about the books and songs I have yet to write,
the stories and poems I will send out into a world,
that might not want me,
I'll play the music that you made and shared,
that you sang into our our hearts,
even here, down under, in wee Aotearoa.
I want to say that it doesn't matter what the world says about me,
or what those bastards said about you,
and every other woman with a truth and a voice,
and God help us when we were given a microphone.
I will use all those rejection letters to light my fires on winter nights,
as my dog snores on the couch,
and the last glass and a half of cabernet something or other,
stares at me from a glowering bottle,
before I tip its last drop into my smeary tumbler of misspent joy;
the one that started off as fun,
but later will become the headache of elusive fame,
in the morning after,
when I stare at all those clever lines from the night before.
Yet sleep still comes to me,
and like stars in the night sky, I twinkle myself into a big bed of dreaminess,
 my solitary, comfortable nest full of my own compassion,

and the dreamy wanderings,
that I share with imaginary, wordy bedfellows,
who are buried beneath my sweaty sheets, next to the dog.
I tuck myself in and tell myself,
I will go back to the sea tomorrow and gather more
stories and songs to bring home
to bind up into my beautiful life that is not for sale,
or to become pickings for a carnal, snarling, unbelieving world.
I will carry my legacy home from the beach,
and leave it on the shelf with my memories,
the framed photos of everyone I ever lost,
and the souls I managed to keep.
Then later on when I am gone, just like you, Sinead,
and every other woman that ever had a truth and a voice,
and if we were lucky, a microphone.
all the world will read or listen to the words we left behind
and they will all say, "she was pretty good, aye?
No wonder she was famous."

RIP Sinead – *now you can, "sleep with a clear conscience, you can sleep in peace".*

REQUIEM FOR A PIKELET

Here are some of the poems, old and new that I have written over the past 40 years - *For Linda xx*

Visit Lyn today (1986)

With blue sky overhead,
sunshine in my pocket,
sandals on my feet,
I hitchhiked to the beach –
to see a friend.
A week later, my sunshine used up,
the blue turned to grey sky
my sandals broken & dusty –
I borrowed a jersey
and caught the bus home.
(Golden Bay 1986)

Bon voyage Pikelet (1988)

You know my thoughts,
you sense my feelings and sometimes
you just turn up at my door,
in my house with smiles and kisses,
arms waiting to embrace me.
But you are going away now, and I feel hollow –
so hollow like a donut without cream.
I will pray for your safety,
that no green-lipped boogie man eats you.
Your face shall be a rare feast on the continent,
a shadowy ache in my mind.
I shall whisper, Pikelet to no one,
dancing alone in the dark in a tiny room.
When I see zebra crossings,
black and white, those are your favourite colours.
You will never escape my missile thoughts,
of love piercing time and oceans, sky and trains.

Funny as Pikelets & Donuts (2019)

I'm not sure how to start
to talk about you and all the crazy,
crazy times
that made the memories for our kids
so solid and unforgettable.
Our music,
the soundtrack of their childhoods.
Our dancing to be feared.
Our clothes??
An embarrassing, colourful, style -
fashion not...
and then the hair,
the photos,
gaudy cars and road trips,
baking, drinking,
late nights with strangers
and so many, more beloved friends,
that kept the kids awake.

Back when we thought about heaven
but not very much,
not enough to sleep inside our prayers at night.
Back then
all there was to think about was the next sunny ride,
a pretty dress to wear,
hefty, tasty home-cooked meals
followed by pikelets and donuts.
You and Me,
with our kids tucked up,
sort of, late at night.
If only I could turn the clock back
a couple of hours
where I could grab your hand.
I would pull you off that bus
out of that car,
block your path to martyrdom.
Call me selfish.
I wish that you were still here
on the end of my bed
reading me some sh*t poem that maybe I had written
and we couldn't stop laughing, and started crying
at me and our stupid selves.
Now that was crying from a good time.

In the stillness I find you God

In the stillness, not as I walk or run nor when I sit or lie down inside the quiet, waiting for a voice from nowhere.

In that stillness where nothing else exists... no rain from Heaven, sun or falling stars on the ground with gentle dust upon my feet.

The stillness in my heart that keeps a light on inside the space reserved for you. Somewhere in that stillness most days, God, I find you.

The Light in my Heart

There is a light in my heart,
that searches for you,
in a dark place of loss
where the earth no longer holds colour,
only shadows of a thousand yesterdays
while faint laughter carries across eternity
teasing my memories.
The light in my heart listens,
for that song rolling out on the radio,
notes and lyrics pulling me back to those days of
dancing, leaping, shouting,
our spontaneity making the kitchen a dance floor of
sweat, laughter, alcohol, heartbeats, more.
The light in my heart holds,
my last email to you,
the final poem I wrote,
a shirt that you made for me,
black and gold, too small now,
and a handful of photos, of you always smiling,
always dressed up, colourful and gay,

happy beside me.
The light in my heart remembers,
all the times you stayed with me,
the houses that we lived in,
parties, dinners, all night raves and movies.
Every single place we ever went,
the footpaths where we ambled arm in arm,
children running ahead,
a cat, a dog,
added company for our lives.
That light in my heart now cries,
for all the days we shared,
the nights we would hang out together.
I can still feel the tendrils of longing
for the months we spent apart,
shivering despair, for the years where I lost you.
and the wonder of finding you,
all over again,
after so many, many years.
Then one ordinary Friday morning in autumn
across 19 minutes
the news tore my soul
as I teetered on a furious knife edge of disbelief,
My tears raining like bullets,
your flame was extinguished,
my joy indefinitely muted and quashed.
Five years later,
it's once again another ordinary Friday morning in autumn.
But I hold my breathe and cry for those 19 minutes

that destroyed the love,
and took away,
the light in my heart that was you.

ACKNOWLEDGEMENTS

Once again, huge love and thanks to my friends and my sons who support and cheer me on. To my Mum who has become one of my biggest fans following the success of my first book, "The Long Cold Nights of June."

Mum never misses my talks and sells my books alongside her famous preserves and pickles at all the farmers markets that she attends here in Doubtless Bay, and wider Northland area of New Zealand.

Lastly, hugs and so much love to Ange Armstrong who lost her Mum in the Linwood Mosque Shootings of 2019. Our chats and sharing of photos and memories of Linda have been so precious to me. Linda, a.k.a Pikelet, was always going to be in this book but now she has her own chapter and just like in life, her name and story are now held in Heaven.

God bless y'all and see you in the next book!

About the author

Debby Curreen has spent most of her adult life the Far North of NZ, mainly in the Mangonui/ Doubtless Bay area. Debby is strongly connected to the Far North and is of Irish, Māori and English decent . She is a mum and grandma.

Debby started self-publishing in 2018 with a poetry collection called, 'The Long Cold Nights of June' telling her story of healing after her youngest brother died from suicide in 2006. She published another collection of poems in 2020 and a short story collection in 2022 called 'Break all my falls' which has uniquely New Zealand themes with some of the stories interconnecting. Debby published one more collection of poems at the end of 2022 before beginning to write her novel due out in 2024/25.

Debby has had poems included in several Northland anthologies and more recently in Iona Winter's 'Liminal Gathering' almanac in 2023. Debby regularly holds regular Spoken Word & Poetry workshops where she enjoys encouraging other writers on their writing journeys.

In her spare time, Debby enjoys the beach, her dogs, sharing meals and a glass of local red wine with family and friends, gardening and reading, and live music especially if her sons and friends are playing.

www.ingramcontent.com/pod-product-compliance
Lightning Source LLC
Chambersburg PA
CBHW031301290426
44109CB00012B/668